BEER CART LANE   CHANGES AT THE OLD BREWERY SITE

This photograph taken in October 1956 shows a Salvation Army march past and parade, no doubt heading for their headquarters in nearby White Horse Lane.

Although not the main subject of the photograph at the time, of more significance now are the buildings along Beer Cart Lane in the background. This rarely photographed lane has seen many changes along its south side in the last thirty years. Originally, this group of buildings was a brewery, hence the name Beer Cart Lane. At the time this photograph was taken, the buildings around the yard to the right belonged to Allred Distributors of no. 1 Beer Cart Lane. Further to the left at no. 2 was the premises of GEC, and out of sight at no. 3 was the yard of L.T. Dadds, builders. In 1967, LES Distributors took over from GEC at no. 2.

In October 1971 planning permission was granted to construct the four-storey office block we see today. It was about this time that the old warehouses, stores and garages were demolished. Building work was started towards the end of 1972, and completed during the following year. The new building contains the Canterbury registry office and is witness to a continual stream of weddings. The empty site on the opposite corner in the 1956 picture once contained a row of buildings that continued down Stour Street to Hawks Lane. Regrettably, they were destroyed in the blitz of June 1942, although traces of some of the old buildings can still be seen in the walls around Wiltshiers yard, particularly towards Hawks Lane.

(Kentish Gazette)

CASTLE STREET   BEFORE THE RING ROAD CAME

This fascinating photograph dates from Spring 1960, and shows the top of Castle Street from its junction with Wincheap. The road veering off to the right is Wincheap Green which then leads into Pin Hill.

This seemingly deserted road junction and many of the surrounding buildings disappeared between 1961 and 1963 to make way for the Wincheap roundabout. This new roundabout is at the Wincheap end of the 'Rheims Way' dual carriageway, or the A2 diversion, as it was referred to in the planning stages.

The changes began in the summer of 1961 with the demolition of the terraced houses on the left of the photograph, and just beyond the junction with Wincheap Grove. These, and similar ones in Wincheap Grove itself, disappeared earlier than other affected buildings to allow the construction of an embankment for the planned dual carriageway. The earth for this was moved from a similar embankment in nearby Wincheap, which had once supported the Elham Valley railway line. The embankment would enable the new road to follow a level route away from the site of the planned roundabout.

Other buildings were demolished in 1963, only months before the Rheims Way was opened. These included the 'Castle Hotel' on the right of the picture.

Beyond the now lost buildings are the doctors' surgery on the right and the Norman Castle keep on the left. Today, these buildings mark the upper limit of Castle Street. Since its construction, the roundabout has been re-modelled several times in an effort to improve traffic flow. Future plans may include an underpass beneath the existing roundabout, for traffic passing from Pin Hill straight onto the Rheims Way.

(Fisk-Moore Studio)

A fine study of the Castle Street frontage of the 'Castle Hotel', as seen from the junction of Wincheap Grove opposite. The hotel was originally built following a rough triangular design, with another frontage, onto Wincheap Green, hidden from the camera. The spire of St Andrew's Presbyterian Church can be seen jutting above the roof of the hotel.

The 'Castle Hotel' was demolished in 1963 to make way for the roundabout that joined the new Rheims Way into the existing road system. The former site of the hotel would now be in the centre of the Wincheap roundabout.
(Kentish Gazette)

No. 28 Castle Street, the doctors' surgery building, survives today and is situated right on the edge of the Wincheap roundabout. The photograph was taken in the spring of 1961 from an upper storey window of the British Road Services building opposite. It offers an interesting glimpse into the surgery's private walled garden, much of which was taken for the construction of the aforementioned roundabout. No. 28 Castle Street was built into the city wall, adjacent to the site of the Roman Worthgate. It also cleverly imitates the medieval city wall bastion that once stood on this site.

(Bill Entwhistle)

Another general view of the much-changed area, this time looking up Castle Street and into Wincheap. From this angle, familiar features that survive today can be seen, including the Wincheap railway bridge and the 'Man of Kent' public house, then known as the 'Station Hotel'.

This photograph also dates from spring 1961, with the now long since demolished buildings on the right casting shadows in the spring sunshine. The three-storey building on the extreme right is the premises of the Canterbury branch of British Road Services. As with the 'Castle Hotel', this building was demolished in 1963 to make way for the Rheims Way.
(Bill Entwhistle)

GRAVEL WALK (1)   THE MEDIEVAL WALL OF WHITEFRIARS

Gravel Walk has changed completely in the last thirty years, from being a quiet, narrow city lane to a wide and busy thoroughfare. Moreover, every building on both sides was demolished between the years 1960 and 1965.

The photograph above was taken in early 1960 and shows the ancient Whitefriars perimeter wall running down the north side of Gravel Walk and round into Rose Lane in the foreground. Behind the wall are the grounds of the old Simon Langton Boys' School, which had closed a few months earlier, in November 1959. The building that can be seen further up Gravel Walk is the old school's science block (see pages 26 and 27), now standing empty. Originally, both boys' and girls' Simon Langton Schools were situated at the Whitefriars, the site of a medieval friary. However, the girls' school re-located shortly after the Canterbury blitz, when much of the Whitefriars complex was destroyed. By the time the picture was taken the boys' school had moved into their new school premises at Nackington.

The empty school buildings and the old perimeter wall were demolished during June and July of 1960. The cleared site was subsequently used for the widening of Gravel Walk and St George's Lane, the provision of a surface car park and the construction of Ricemans and 'The Coach and Horses'. The 'now' photograph shows the widened and re-aligned junction of Gravel Walk with Rose Lane, as well as the Whitefriars Shopping Centre on the left, which had replaced the surface car park in 1972.

However, the fairly new shopping centre may itself soon be demolished, as part of the re-think of some of the post war redevelopment sites. These also include the Longmarket and St George's clock tower sites.

(Fisk-Moore Studio)

The Fisk-Moore photographic study of the old Simon Langton School site in early 1960 was quite comprehensive. Over twenty different views were taken, and many will surface in 'Then and Now' articles and books in the near future. This picture shows the other side of the ancient Whitefriars perimeter wall around the junction of Rose Lane and Gravel Walk beyond. There is much medieval building material in evidence, as well as areas of red-brick marking later repair work. The wall also appears to have been raised in height, also in red-brick. The structure on the left is one of the many recently vacated pre-fabricated buildings of the boys' school.

(Fisk-Moore Studio)

Also from the 1960 survey, this picture shows some of the pre-fabricated buildings in that corner of the Simon Langton School grounds enclosed by the old perimeter wall. These pre-fabs, and a number of others, were erected following the heavy losses sustained by the Langton School in the blitz of June 1942. As mentioned opposite, the boys' school stayed on at the Whitefriars site, using both the surviving buildings and the pre-fabs.

The large brick building in the centre background is the office buildings adjacent to Williams coach builders that stood on the south side of Gravel Walk at the Rose Lane end. The bare winter trees are the same ones as in the opposite photograph.

(Fisk-Moore Studio)

This photograph dates from May 1968, and was taken from roughly the same place as the view above. It shows a much changed scene, with only the Marlowe Theatre common to both pictures. The old Simon Langton School complex had been demolished in 1960, and Gravel Walk widened in 1963. The buildings on the far side of Gravel Walk had disappeared by 1966.

The Whitefriars surface car park in the foreground was one of a number in the area providing acres of much needed parking at the time, along Gravel Walk, Rose Lane and Watling Street.

The inner city parking policy of the 1960s was contrary to that of the 1990s, with the gradual emergence of park and ride areas outside of Canterbury.

(Kentish Gazette)

THE GUILDHALL   A LOST CANTERBURY TREASURE

Throughout the last war, many decisions affecting Canterbury were made at monthly meetings of the city council at the Guildhall. Even the planned meeting of 3rd June 1942 went ahead, despite it being just two days after the infamous Baedeker raid. And yet, just five years after the end of the war, the building had gone.

There had been a Guildhall on the site for many centuries, and substantial remains of a medieval timber framed building existed behind the later facade. This facade, very much in the same neo-classical style as the old pre-war Longmarket building, was constructed in two stages. The frontage onto the High Street at the front dated from the early nineteenth century. A matching facade onto Guildhall Street was built around a century later. Unfortunately, some of this work was botched, although it looked splendid.

By 1950, the Guildhall was in serious danger of collapse, and would have cost an estimated £18,000 to renovate and make safe. This was considered to be too much by the then powers that be, and despite the Guildhall's history and importance, it was demolished. The Kentish Gazette summed up the feelings of many Canterbury citizens by saying:. 'The decision to demolish the building was made and carried out with unseemly haste, and represents the sacrifice of an object of great antiquity on the altar of modernity'.

However, not all of the ancient Guildhall has been lost. Some of the interior fittings were transferred to the new Guildhall in the former Holy Cross Church. Furthermore, the modern shoe shop now on the site of the old Guildhall hides an ancient secret. This is further explained on the opposite page.

(Fisk-Moore Studio)

The interior of the old Guildhall is truly a lost treasure. This historical chamber was the scene of countless public ceremonies dating back to at least 1438. It is known that even in the fourteenth century there was a guild or city hall at the same location, then virtually in the middle of medieval Canterbury. Furthermore, there is reason to believe that the site was the headquarters of the merchants' guild in the twelfth century. In more recent years, the city council had met here under the leadership of Catherine Williamson and Charles Lefevre, and had debated and decided on vital policies affecting Canterbury in the Second World War.

(Fisk-Moore Studio)

The demolition of the Guildhall in 1950 took the building down to within approximately twelve feet from the ground, as this early 1950's photograph clearly shows. Presumably, this was to avoid the need to erect a fence or hoardings around the site, to secure it prior to redevelopment. The picture also shows a new party wall being built against the adjoining timber framed building. The unsafe condition of the Guildhall structure had had an adverse effect on this adjoining shop, so I expect the owners were glad to be rid of the potential danger.

(Messenger group newspapers)

The remaining ground floor walls of the Guildhall survived until 1955, when the site was totally cleared prior to redevelopment. During this demolition and clearance work, a remarkably fine twelfth century stone column was discovered amongst the foundations. It was thought to be the central support column of a groined vault, erected in about 1190. There would have been four further columns giving support at each corner. The vault itself, together with the four corner columns, were removed in around 1500, during re-modelling work. Fortunately, the central support column survived this, and all successive re-building works. Moreover, it still survives today, preserved *in situ*, within the foundations of the shoe shop built on the site of the old Guildhall in 1956. It would be interesting to known if this ancient column can be viewed.

(Kentish Gazette)

LONGMARKET (1)
THE GRADUAL DEMOLITION OF A NEO-CLASSICAL GATEWAY

One of the most important commercial buildings to be destroyed as a result of the blitz in June 1942 was the Longmarket and Corn Exchange. Built in 1825, in a neo-classical style, this magnificent structure ran from its main entrance in The Parade along to a smaller, rear entrance gateway in Burgate.

Unfortunately, like so many buildings in the St George's area, the Longmarket and Corn Exchange building fell victim to a hail of incendiary bombs that resulted in a massive conflagration. Most of the burnt out shell of the building was demolished in the summer of 1942, but two sections survived and were retained, lasting well into the 1950s. One part, at The Parade and St George's Street end, was Hamilton's Wine Merchants (see pages 16 and 17). The other surviving part, pictured here, was the aforementioned rear entrance gateway, which also encompassed public lavatories.

The photograph was taken around 1957, just after demolition had begun. This involved dismantling the central gateway and right hand portion of the structure only. The left hand part was reprieved for a number of months before it too was demolished.

The 'now' picture was taken in the autumn of 1989, and appeared in the Kentish Gazette feature shortly afterwards. The Fudge Shop on the right is part of the 1961 Longmarket development. In the early 1990s we will see yet another redevelopment of the site, when these box-like structures will be replaced by buildings in a pastiche of older styles.

Although the old neo-classical gateway is long gone, the two stone plaques depicting the city arms, seen on either side of the entrance, still survive. They are now part of the city's collection, and today, one of them can be seen in the entrance hall to the Heritage Museum in Stour Street.

(Fisk-Moore Studio)

8

This much earlier photograph of the Long-market dates from 1949, and shows some of the recently constructed pre-fabricated shops. Those in the picture stand on the site of the old Longmarket and Corn Exchange building, destroyed by fire in June 1942. The surviving gateway to and from Burgate can be seen beyond the pre-fabs and the shoppers keenly surveying the new premises. This block of pre-fabricated shops was the first to be dismantled when the site was completely cleared in 1959.
(Fisk-Moore Studio)

Another picture of the old neo-classical gate-way during its partial demolition, seen from the Longmarket, looking out into Burgate. This work was requested by tenants of the Longmarket pre-fab shops in June 1956, and carried out when modern replacement lavatories in Canterbury Lane were ready. The part of the gateway structure to be temporarily retained is on the right of the picture. This lasted until the end of 1958 when it too was demolished.

(Fisk-Moore Studio)

This photograph dates from around November 1958, and is from roughly the same position as the picture opposite. By this time the retained portion of the gateway had been dismantled, and little of it remained other than a pile of rubble seen on the left. In a few months' time the pre-fabricated shops in the centre of the picture would be demolished, to allow free access to the new row of shops recently completed on the left.

(Fisk-Moore Studio)

9

BURGATE LANE
THE LOST BUILDINGS OF A MUCH CHANGED LANE

Burgate Lane is one of the five lanes running in parallel from Burgate Street to the main thoroughfare of The Parade and St George's Street. The others are Mercery Lane, Butchery Lane, Iron Bar Lane and Canterbury Lane. All but Mercery Lane suffered in the blitz of June 1942, as the old parish of St George's burnt to the ground. However, Burgate Lane was not the worst affected, and many of its buildings survived the blitz. Despite this, only two of those surviving buildings can be seen today. One is a tiny shop at the Burgate end, and the other is Zoar Chapel which can be seen in the right of the picture.

Zoar Chapel is a much remodelled 'D' shaped bastion in the city wall. It dates from 1845 and was built for the strict Baptist denomination. Today, it is still used as a non-conformist chapel. The St George's Street end of Burgate Lane, nearest the camera, suffered badly in the June 1942 blitz, and the post-war re-building was slow to reach the area. By the time the photograph was taken in July 1959, most of the Lane's surviving buildings were still standing, although a row of cottages opposite Zoar Chapel had recently been demolished.

The main subject of the picture was originally the excavation undertaken by the Electricity Board, but now the lost buildings beyond are of much more interest.

Today, Burgate Lane is a much changed, but nevertheless pleasant, thoroughfare containing some interesting modern shops. However, the largest of the new buildings opposite the chapel was much criticised when new in 1974, for being an 'eyesore'. There are certainly much worse eyesores in Canterbury. It was also criticised for blocking the view of the cathedral; an accusation levelled against many new buildings since post-war redevelopment began.

(Fisk-Moore Studio)

This photograph was taken in January 1959 from the end of a newly re-modelled St George's Terrace. Burgate Lane can be seen on the other side of the main street. At the junction of Burgate Lane, the main street changed from St George's Street into St George's Gate from left to right. Empty bomb sites are still very much in evidence along the St George's Gate section. This would remain as such for another ten years, until the construction of St George's roundabout.

The new buildings on the left are the latest in the spread of redevelopment along the main street.

(John Martin)

Another picture from July 1959 features the Seeboard excavations in Burgate Lane. The large building on the right is the old Co-operative premises that fronted onto Lower Bridge Street (see pages 20 and 21). The excavation work necessitated the demolition of a large section of the rear of this building. It can be seen in a more complete state in the above photograph which dates from earlier in 1959. Once the roadworks had been completed the southern end of Burgate Lane was re-modelled in a similar fashion to the north end of St George's Terrace opposite. In addition to this, the stretch of city wall from Zoar Chapel down to St George's Gate was reconstructed in flint.

(Fisk-Moore Studio)

The southern end of Burgate Lane was modernised and redeveloped from 1959 on-wards. New shops can new be seen in this south-facing photograph, which dates from the summer of 1966. The rest of Burgate Lane hung in limbo for much of the 1960s, with the old buldings on both sides of the lane, between Zoar Chapel and Burgate, becoming increasingly more ruinous. Demolition was piecemeal, as each old building became vacant. By the time the photograph was taken, the scene recalled the immediate post-war years else-where in Canterbury, with empty and over-grown sites alternating with the remaining buildings. The vast majority of the old properties had gone by the end of the decade.

(Ben May)

DOVER STREET
THE COMING AND GOING OF THE BLIGH BROS GARAGES

This typical 1950's street scene was captured by the Fisk-Moore studio in the summer of 1959. The main subject of the photograph is the Dover Street premises of Bligh Bros Limited, known as Star Garage. The firm also had premises in St Radigund's Street. At the time, Bligh Bros had been trading in Canterbury for almost 150 years. They were established in 1812 and prospered in the early nineteenth century, building a variety of horse-drawn vehicles. In the early 1900s they turned to making motor car bodies. During the First World War they produced artillery wheels for military vehicles. The 1930s and 1940s were lean years for the firm, but recovery came in the post-war years. By 1959 Bligh Brothers had twelve branches throughout East Kent.

Towards the end of the 1950s the Dover Street garage had become too small and antiquated to cope with the 'never had it so good' years, with car ownership very much on the increase. Consequently, the cottages seen on the left of the garage were purchased, demolished and the cleared site used to construct a new garage. The modern premises incorporated garage area, showrooms, office accommodation and a petrol pump forecourt.

However, the new garage complex has itself since been demolished, as the 'now' photograph clearly demonstrates. Nevertheless, this area has not seen the last of the changes. The current city local plan shows the existing car parking area long Dover Street designated for residential development. Therefore, we will soon come full circle, with the return of the residential dwellings to the site.

(Fisk-Moore Studio)

12

This is a general view of the western end of Dover Street, also dating from the summer of 1959. It was taken from the 'new' stretch of city wall, then currently being constructed between St George's Gate and the Riding Gate. The sixteenth century 'Flying Horse' can clearly be seen here. It was badly damaged in the blitz of Canterbury, particularly the roof, and was at one time threatened with demolition. Luckily, it was rebuilt in the immediate post-war years. The empty plot on the opposite corner of Dover Street was also as a result of enemy action.

(Fisk-Moore Studio)

Five cottages stood between the old Bligh Brothers garage and the 'Nag's Head Inn'. This photograph was taken at the end of 1959 and shows the lost Dover Street cottages just prior to demolition. Between the years 1959 and 1966 many such terraced houses in Canterbury succumbed to the bulldozer, usually following compulsory purchase. Most were demolished in the various slum clearance programmes, whilst others such as these, still sound in construction, gave way to new developments. However, compulsory purchase was not necessary in this case. Bligh Brothers purchased these cottages one by one until every one was owned by them.

(Fisk-Moore Studio)

This photograph dates from December 1960 and was taken just prior to the official opening of the new premises. Designed by architects Dudley Marsh and Partners, the new garage and showrooms were opened by the Mayor, Councillor Tom McCallum. The picture could also be subject to a 'Then and Now' feature for, as mentioned opposite, the new premises have since been demolished. Little remains of the modern garage, except some wall fragments round the back of the site, including an overgrown doorway leading to nowhere.

(Kentish Gazette)

DUCK LANE   THE HOUSES THAT GAVE WAY TO A CAR PARK

Slum clearance in the 1960s was widespread across much of Britain, as councils and authorities attempted to improve the living conditions of the people who occupied these so-called slums. Canterbury played its part in this process, and demolished many late eighteenth and nineteenth century houses. Many of these stood in the Northgate and St Radigund's areas of the city. In the former area, demolition sites were quickly re-developed with modern housing, but in the latter, the old houses gave way to provide valuable inner city car parking areas.

This picture dates from April 1964 and shows Duck Lane from the junction with St Radigund's Street. It was at about this time that the occupants along the north side of Duck Lane, and in the adjoining St Radigund's Place, were progressively rehoused. Following the eventual demolition of these houses, further and more extensive clearance of the area was planned in the wake of the proposed third phase of the ring road. This would have flattened much of Broad Street, St Radigund's Street and North Lane. The scheme was finally abandoned, with mixed feelings, in 1975.

Fortunately, the south side of Duck Lane exists today, and is an attractive row of renovated cottages. The north side contains the Duck Lane surface car park and, although the houses have long since gone, the original pavement and a few well foundations can still be seen.

Many of Canterbury's surface car parks are now designated for future residential development, including the one here at Duck Lane. However, the larger parking area adjacent to this one between the former St Radigund's Place and the River Stour, will remain as a surface car park into the foreseeable future.

(Kentish Gazette)

This photograph dates from April 1964 and was taken much further down Duck Lane. All the houses appear to be occupied at the time, but it would not be long before the residents would be rehoused. Most of them went to different parts of the city, particularly to the new housing estates, then mushrooming around the outskirts of Canterbury. The vast majority of the new estates were laid out with conventional streets and houses, fortunately avoiding the high-rise building policies of larger cities.

(Kentish Gazette)

Two years later the now empty and forlorn-looking terraced houses of Duck Lane were not far off demolition. This picture was taken by Ben May in the spring of 1966, employing a wider-angled lens than the one used for the opposite photograph. At the time there was a chronic shortage of car parking spaces in Canterbury. Slum clearance in the St Radigund's area provided the city with two modest-sized car parks. As well as the one in Duck Lane, the St Radigund's Street car park was also created (see pages 22 and 23).

(Ben May)

Another photograph from the spring of 1966, featuring the other end of Duck Lane. Just beyond the picture on the left was St Radigund's Place, a name that no longer appears on the map, as all of its houses were demolished later in 1966. The building partly hidden from view by the tree on the right is the end house of the south side of Duck Lane. This, and all the terraced houses along the south elevation, survive today. In the centre of the photograph is no. 18 Duck Lane, that had been badly damaged by fire in August 1965.

(Ben May)

LONGMARKET (2)
THE WINE MERCHANTS IN PART OF THE OLD LONGMARKET

At the time of writing, the Longmarket is about to undergo a major change, with the demolition of the existing early 1960s buildings. Older Canterbury citizens will remember that the Longmarket has twice before been demolished and redeveloped in the last fifty years. The first such occasion was just after 1st June 1942, when much of the burnt out shell of the late Georgian Corn Exchange and Longmarket buildings was demolished. The blitz of Canterbury also displaced many small businesses along St George's Street and Burgate and, in the late 1940s, prefabricated shops were built on much of the old Longmarket site for their benefit.

The photograph dates from around June 1956 and shows the Longmarket area in a transitional state, with old, temporary and new buildings represented. The curiously-shaped brick building in the foreground on the right is the premises of J.H.G. Hamilton wine merchants. This structure is a surviving part of the blitzed Longmarket building, and the round-topped arches seen on its side once extended along the inside of the old market hall.

The temporary buildings are the aforementioned pre-fabricated shops which dominated the scene throughout the 1950s. The new building is the National Provincial Bank which would open for business in July 1956. During the same month Hamiltons, together with the bank's own pre-fab next to it, were demolished.

The remaining pre-fabs were progressively dismantled throughout 1959. The new development that subsequently emerged will also have been demolished by the time this book appears. However, the row of shops stretching from the bank down to Athena will be retained at least for now.

(Fisk-Moore Studio)

16

A ground level view of Hamilton wine merchants taken from The Parade, at the same time as the picture opposite. The frontage of the pre-war Longmarket building would have extended across the entire area of the photograph. Its ground floor elevation consisted of the three round-topped arches into the central Longmarket trading area, flanked by small rectangular retail frontages. Hamiltons had the right hand retail section, and this was the only piece to survive the blitz. In fact, the post-war Hamiltons originally retained an actual section of the classical frontage, complete with one neo-classical column, but this was removed in the early 1950s.

(Fisk-Moore Studio)

The remainder of the old Hamilton premises was demolished in July 1956, and this photograph shows that work in progress. The newly constructed National Provincial Bank building behind soars above it, and surely caused the demise of this relic of the blitz. A buddleia shrub, very much associated with the early post-war years of Canterbury, can be seen growing out of the brickwork.

(Kentish Gazette)

This photograph dates from around January 1959 and was taken from the same vantage point as the picture opposite. By this time J.H.G. Hamilton was trading from the National Provincial Bank building and the area once occupied by their old premises had been neatly tarmac'ed over. However, the old wine merchant premises could be likened to an iceberg, in that most of it existed below the surface. Underneath the old Hamilton's was a large wine cellar, and when the ground floor structure was demolished, another access staircase was constructed from their new premises in the bank building. Thus, the old cellar continued in use until Hamiltons finally ceased trading. It survived the redevelopment of the Longmarket in 1960 and 1961, and still survives to this day.

(Fisk-Moore Studio)

HIGH STREET ST GREGORY
THE MYSTERY OF A LANE WITH A HIGH ST NAME

The name 'High Street St Gregory' is a curious one for a short and narrow lane that runs between Northgate and Victoria Row. The 'St Gregory' part is easily explained as the lane traverses the site once occupied by the twelfth century St Gregory's Priory. In fact, it crosses exactly where the priory's bell tower once stood. Unfortunately, this prevented the tower's foundations from being thoroughly excavated in the recent extensive archaeological dig of the priory site either side of High Street St Gregory.

The 'High Street' part, however, is not so straightforward, and was the subject of much debate on the letters page of the Kentish Gazette in 1961. This arose because members of the nearby St Gregory's Church appealed for the mystery of the name to be solved, before High Street St Gregory disappeared under planned redevelopment proposals. Various ideas were put forward, including a suggestion that it was named as

such, because it was an important thoroughfare in the nineteenth century, with many small shops and businesses. Regretfully, none of the suggestions seemed convincing.

The photograph of High Street St Gregory dates from January 1961 and looks towards Victoria Row, where the charming white house can be seen. On the far left are the terraced houses along the north side of Artillery Street, soon to disappear (see pages 30 and 31). The central block of dwellings which included Artillery Street south side, the aforementioned white house, and the terrace to the right of it in Artillery Gardens, lasted until the mid 1960s.

Redevelopment plans must have been altered as High Street St Gregory survives to this day, with the same cobbled edges visible in 1961.

(Kentish Gazette)

Another view of High Street St Gregory from January 1961, but looking in the opposite direction towards Northgate. The 'Model Tavern' in Northgate can just be seen through the gap. The void on the right was as a result of blitz damage. This site would subsequently be used for the construction of the Northgate sorting office. Beyond this is the back of the 'Two Brothers' public house. This closed in 1966 but the building survived and was recently extensively renovated. On the left beyond the garage is a row of old buildings, many of which were subsequently demolished to make way for the sorting office car park.

(Kentish Gazette)

Although a number of photographs of High Street St Gregory were taken by the Gazette in January 1961, none were actually used in the newspaper until a 'Then and Now' article in December 1989. This view looks across an empty void recently created by the demolition of much of Artillery Gardens (see pages 38 and 39). The terraced houses in the distance on the left are in Albion Place. They would manage to survive the 1960s demolition schemes which saw the end of many similar types of property.

(Kentish Gazette)

This fascinating view of the Northgate area was taken from the cathedral in December 1980. High Street St Gregory runs horizontally across the centre of the picture with the North-gate sorting office complex on its far side. This 1960s development was demolished in 1988 and an archaeological dig undertaken to discover the remains of the old St Gregory's Priory. The old sorting office car park towards the bottom left of the picture was also excavated. Here, some 1,250 skeletons were discovered from what was once part of the Priory graveyard.

(Kentish Gazette)

19

LOWER BRIDGE STREET (1)
THE OLD CO-OP BUILDING ON A BUSY CROSSROADS

St George's roundabout has been in existence now for just over twenty years. It is a vital part of Canterbury's busy yet incomplete inner ring road. You can imagine, or perhaps remember, how busy the junction was before 1969 when, as a crossroads controlled by traffic lights, it had to cope with local as well as through traffic. St George's crossroads had buildings on three of its corners, and the old cattle market on the fourth.

This photograph was taken in April 1961 and shows the corner between St George's Gate and Lower Bridge Street at St George's cross-roads. The two buildings featured both survived the blitz with only minor damage, whilst those on either side of them were completely destroyed. The large building on the right is the Co-operative store at nos. 11 and 12 Lower Bridge Street. At the time it was pictured, the building was empty and in the process of being demolished. The Co-op subsequently moved into new premises in Burgate Lane just behind. This has since been taken over by C&A and can clearly be seen in the 'now' photograph.

The old Co-operative building started life in 1915 as the St George's theatre and cinema. It replaced a previous building on the site known as St George's livery stables. In 1934 the St George's cinema was super-ceded by the Regal in nearby St George's Place, most of which survives today as the Cannon Cinema.

The old Co-op was demolished some eight years before the St George's roundabout was constructed, and the site became a temporary surface car park for the duration.

The smaller building on the left is the premises of Pettit and Son, tobacconist and stationer. Their address was no. 1 St George's Gate and the buildings survived until 1969, when the roundabout was built. The street name of St George's Gate also disappeared at this time, because this section of road between Burgate Lane and Lower Bridge Street was swallowed up by the roundabout.

(Kentish Gazette)

The old Co-operative building in happier days. This splendid night time photograph dates from June 1953 and shows the Co-op decorated and illuminated to commemorate the coronation of the Queen. Many other shop premises and businesses were likewise decorated, and a number of these were photographed for posterity by the Fisk-Moore Studio. Being positioned on a busy junction, the decorated Co-operative building would have been seen by many Canterbury citizens as well as people passing through the city.

(Fisk-Moore Studio)

Another photograph of the Co-operative building from April 1961, this time taken from Lower Bridge Street. The small temporary shop to the right of the main building was added after the war, and contained the Co-op store's meat department. The vacant site to the right of the Co-operative building was as a result of blitz damage and extended down to the premises of Tice and Co. Engineers at no. 6 Lower Bridge Street.

The progress of demolition on the old Co-op building can clearly be seen in this view, as can a departing Co-operative van; no doubt retrieving last minute fixtures and fittings.

(Kentish Gazette)

As mentioned opposite, when the Co-op building was demolished, its site and the adjoining vacant bomb site became a temporary surface car park. This view dates from around 1965, with Fords outnumbering other makes. In the background on the left can be seen the Zoar Chapel and the old buildings of Burgate Lane (see pages 10 and 11). The tall buildings towards the right of the view stood along the western side of Lower Bridge Street, and clearly show scars of the blitz of Canterbury. They were subsequently demolished in early 1969 to make way for the second stage of the ring road.

(Fisk-Moore Studio)

21

ABBOTS PLACE   SLUM CLEARANCE IN ST RADIGUND'S

Abbots Place was a long row of terraced houses running parallel to, but behind, another row of houses fronting St Radigund's Street (see page opposite). It could be reached only by foot or two-wheeled transport from Mill Lane, alongside the 'Miller's Arms', or from an alley next to garage premises in St Radigund's Street. The photograph of Abbots Place was taken by Ben May for the city council, and is one of a series depicting the then run down St Radigund's area. It dates from the spring of 1966 and shows the terrace of empty houses in a very dilapidated state. The van on the extreme right of the picture is parked in the backyard of the small garage fronting St Radigund's Street, and the white building in the background is the aforementioned 'Miller's Arms' public house. A large demolition programme in 1966 and 1967 across the entire St Radigund's area meant the end for many terraced houses in Duck Lane (see pages 14 and 15), St Radigund's Place, St Radigund's Street, Mill Lane, King Street and all of those in Abbots Place. From the late 1960s to January 1987 the site became the St Radigund's Street surface car park.

In the early 1970s a new Abbots Place came into existence; coming off the nearby Knotts Lane and running just south and east of the original terrace.

Back on the original site, the surface car park was closed in 1987 and turned over to the Canterbury Archaeological Trust, prior to residential redevelopment. The dig uncovered some interesting finds, including the metals relating to two Roman roads.

Today the site contains a thoughtful and aesthetic collection of dwellings that are a far cry from those pulled down well over twenty years ago.

(Ben May)

This row of terraced houses fronted onto St Radigund's Street. The terrace of Abbots Place was behind these houses and faced in the same direction. The alley through to Abbots Place can be seen on the far left of the photograph. The St Radigund's Street houses were built in the 1820s together with the 'Miller's Arms' public house, just visible at the far end of the terrace. The tree-covered area in the background is the site of Abbots mill, burnt down in 1933. The terraced houses of Abbots Place no doubt took their name from the mill, in whose shadow they were built. This picture dates from April 1964, at a time when the cottages were still occupied. The terrace was demolished around the end of 1966, except for the furthest pair of cottages, adjacent to the 'Miller's Arms'.

(Kentish Gazette)

A further picture looking along the soon to be demolished Abbots Place.

(Ben May)

This January 1987 photograph represents the scene in between the 'Then and Now' views on the opposite page, i.e. after the demolition of Abbots Place and the establishment of the car park, but before the recent residential redevelopment. The 'Miller's Arms' and the two surviving end cottages fronting St Radigund's Street can be seen in the background. The old garage building on the extreme right was demolished by members of the Canterbury Archaeological Trust, shortly after this picture was taken.

(Paul Crampton)

Another photograph dating from Spring 1966 and featuring the doomed shop on the corner of Mill Lane and Abbots Place. The name 'Abbots Place' can be seen on the side wall of the 'Miller's Arms' public house in the background. Demolition started with this shop (furthest from the camera in the picture opposite) and gradually worked its way down the Abbots Place terrace. For many years, the site of the shop was used by the 'Miller's Arms' for the storage of beer casks, and it even sprouted a sizeable tree. In the spring of 1987, the site was used to construct the 'Miller's Arms' hotel extension, which completely filled the gap between the pub and the surviving cottage on the extreme right of the picture.

(Ben May)

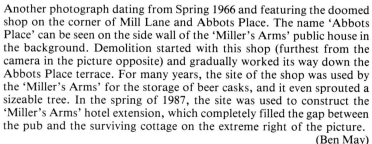

These six photographs were taken from Canterbury Cathedral between the years of 1942 and 1975. They provide a fascinating illustration of the post-war redevelopment of the blitzed St George's part of the city as the modern buildings mushroomed out from the main street and pre-war survivors gradually disappeared under the tide of new development. The first view dates from the autumn of 1942 and shows clearing up operations after the June blitz in an advanced state. Marks and Spencer stands out as the only completely surviving shop in St George's Street.

(Fisk-Moore Studio)

Post-war redevelopment started in 1950. This view from September 1952 shows new buildings emerging on both sides of St George's Street. The north side (nearest the camera) was designated for individual purpose built premises, of which Woolworths on the left (opened July 1952) and Dolcis to its right (opened November 1952) had so far been completed. The first stretch of the Ravenseft terrace of general shops was emerging on the south side. Note the 'intact' ruins of St George's Church, and the two temporary banks to the right of Dolcis.

May 1954 and the north side of St George's Street is really taking shape, with new buildings including W.H. Smith (opened May 1954) and the award winning David Greig just to the right of the clock tower. Loyns bakery in Canterbury Lane is still hanging on, but the two temporary banks have gone, as has the old Kentish Gazette printing works previously to the left of Woolworths. The Ravenseft terrace has extended, and behind it, the Simon Langton school buildings have another six years to go before the bulldozers come.

(Messenger Group Newspapers)

A massive leap forward in time to February 1968, and the Longmarket pre-fabs have given way to the 'shoebox' development (opened October 1961). Other new buildings include Ricemans (opened September 1962) and the 'Coach and Horses' next to it (opened December 1963). A considerable amount of demolition has taken place. The casualties include Loyns Bakery (July 1954), the entire Simon Langton complex at Whitefriars (June 1960), and the many buildings beyond Gravel Walk. Acres of car parking now exist around Gravel Walk, Rose Lane and Watling Street.

(Kentish Gazette)

We have now reached May 1969 and the controversial multi-storey car park is taking shape along the south side of Gravel Walk. It hides the Congregational Church and Marlowe Motors Garage now behind it. St George's Lane does not yet connect to Watling Street, although a vacant strip of land for it can be seen to the left of the emerging multi-storey. The grandiose scheme to build a Civic Centre on the Watling Street car park site had been forgotten by this time, and consequently, the adjacent row of elegant buildings in Dane John was no longer threatened with demolition.

(Kentish Gazette)

September 1975 and the post-war redevelopment of the St George's area and beyond had been completed, the latest major scheme being the Whitefriars shopping centre, finished in 1972. Yet to come in the 1980s would be the Marlowe arcade shopping complex; a new kind of development. It would be carefully designed to look traditional as well as modern, and largely be built of brick and timber.

The 1950s buildings were, on the whole, well designed and an asset to Canterbury. However, the same cannot be said for much of what came in the 1960s and 1970s. Now, a major rethink will result in many of the less well planned developments disappearing; starting with the Longmarket.

(Kentish Gazette)

GRAVEL WALK (2)
THE OLD SIMON LANGTON BOYS' SCHOOL

Having studied one part of the Simon Langton Whitefriars complex on pages 4 and 5, we now move further up Gravel Walk to look at another section of the old school. This early 1960 photograph shows the single storey building at the end of the science block, used as the prefects' room. It was now standing empty following the closure of the old school buildings in November 1959. Former Langton pupil, John Hambrook, remembers often looking through the bow window, as the prefects had a table tennis game inside. The entrance gate seen here was one of two giving access to the school grounds from Gravel Walk. The other was further down towards Rose Lane. Another entrance to the school was from St George's Street through the passage now used as access to the Whitefriars shopping centre.

Beyond the gate in the picture and across Gravel Walk is the premises of Drews Coaches. Until 1942, Drews operated from a garage in Rose Lane, but this was destroyed in the blitz. The firm subsequently leased premises from the council in nearby Gravel Walk, as a temporary measure. They were still there twenty years later, although by now their garage was roofless, and little more than a metal skeleton.

In the summer of 1960, the entire Simon Langton complex at Whitefriars was demolished. By 1964 Gravel Walk had been considerably widened; so much so that the former site of the school's science block was now in the middle of the new road. Drews Garage and all the other buildings along the south side of Gravel Walk were eventually demolished in the mid 1960s.

In October 1966, plans for a multi-storey car park were unveiled. Meanwhile, the site became a surface car park. In fact, the whole area, including Whitefriars and Rose Lane, was one huge surface car park at this time.

Construction of the multi-storey car park finally took place in 1969.
(Fisk-Moore Studio)

The photographs in this feature continue the Fisk-Moore study of the old Simon Langton boys' school, and directly follow on from the pictures featured on pages 4 and 5. This early 1960 view shows the prefects' room from a different angle, and also the adjoining 'chemical laboratory' which was built in 1894. A short stretch of the Whitefriars perimeter wall can be seen beyond the prefects' room on the right.

In the months between the closure of the school and demolition of the buildings, the Simon Langton grounds were sometimes used as a car park.

(Fisk-Moore Studio)

Further along the science block and adjoining the 'chemical laboratory', was the more substantial 'workshop and physical laboratory' dating from 1897. It stood at the top of Gravel Walk at the junction with St George's Lane, although it is pictured here from inside the school grounds.

The entire science block was added to the school under William Partington-Mann, headmaster of Simon Langton Boys' School from 1884 to 1908. His tenure saw the addition of woodwork and art rooms, as well as the science laboratories.

(Fisk-Moore Studio)

This picture dates from August 1962, some two years after the Simon Langton School complex was demolished. The photographer is standing on what is now St George's Lane. Gravel Walk can be seen on the left, with the buildings on its south side from Drews Garage down to the Ministry of Health building still standing at this time. This view would now be blocked by the 'Coach and Horses' public house, which was subsequently built on the corner of a much widened Gravel Walk and re-aligned St George's Lane. This functional hostelry was opened in December 1963.

(Courtesy of Canterbury City Council)

BURGATE   THE DEMISE OF THE 'SARACEN'S HEAD'

The 'Saracen's Head' was an impressive multiple-gabled inn situated just outside the city wall, which it abutted. It stood on the junction of Lower Bridge Street with Burgate. Behind it was a small courtyard sandwiched between the city wall and the inn's outbuildings fronting Lower Bridge Street.

The inn was probably constructed as a house in the seventeenth century, on the site of the city's defensive moat, which had been filled in by this time. Some books have dated it much earlier, as a fifteenth century pilgrims' lodging house. This is unlikely, as the moat would have almost certainly been intact into the sixteenth century. Furthermore, it post-dates the 'Burgate' city gate of 1525, as it was built around the gate's southern tower. From the 1690s onwards, it was definitely an inn called the 'Saracen's Head'; a name it retained until the end.

When the ring road for Canterbury was planned in the early post-war years, it became immediately apparent that this historical building was in the way, and therefore doomed. As long ago as June 1955 the local MP, John Baker White, expressed his personal hope that the 'Saracen's Head' could somehow be saved. Unfortunately, despite many similar pleas over the following years, the inn was demolished in the spring of 1969, to make way for the second phase of the ring road from Wincheap Green to Broad Street. The 'Saracen's Head' is pictured here in February 1969, around the time of its closure and compulsory purchase. Another picture of the inn, in happier times, can be found on page 45.

Today the site is occupied by the second carriageway for Lower Bridge Street and an improved junction into Burgate.

(Kentish Gazette)

This is an earlier view which dates from August 1952, and looks up Burgate Street from the outside of the 'Saracen's Head'. The building in the foreground on the left is the premises of E.R. Bates Motor Repairs, standing between the 'Saracen's Head' and Burgate Lane. It was built in around 1810, originally as two shops, on the former site of the southern tower of the 'Burgate' city gate. The gate's northern tower once adjoined the cottage on the right of the picture (no. 3 Burgate). This tower was demolished later than its southern partner, in 1822. However, fragments of the 'Burgate' northern tower can still be seen forming part of the cottage today.

(Kentish Gazette)

As can be seen here and in the top photograph, Burgate Lane was once considerably narrower than it is today. The pictures date from the summer of 1966, and were taken at a time when Burgate Lane was undergoing piecemeal demolition. (See also page 11.) The building on the right of the upper view joined onto the rear of the E.R. Bates premises, and were constructed at the same time, although originally as two cottages. This building also backed straight on to the medieval city wall, which has since been exposed by its demolition.

(Ben May)

Stage two of the ring road caused the demolition of the 'Saracen's Head' and the adjoining premises of E.R. Bates which was, by then, known as Burgate Motors. The photograph dates from the spring of 1969 and shows Burgate Motors in an advanced state of demolition. Remains of the 'Saracen's Head' can also be seen in the background, still attached to the city wall. Soon after, the city wall flintwork was cleaned of any seventeenth and eighteenth century brickwork, so that no trace of these once significant buildings can now be found.

(Bernard Odden)

ARTILLERY STREET
THE OPPOSITION TO 1960s COMPULSORY PURCHASE

This photograph dates from June 1960 and shows the north side of Artillery Street; that is the left side with the camera towards the Military Road end. It was commissioned by the Canterbury City Council, as these houses were subject to a compulsory purchase and clearance order. Slum clearance in the Northgate area was carried out in stages, taking each row or block of properties at a time. In most cases, this was immediately followed by residential redevelopment, again in stages. Areas already demolished by this time included the eastern side of Military Road and the block between New Ruttington Lane and the north side of Union Street.

The compulsory purchase order in question this time covered the block between Union Street (south side) and Artillery Street, and therefore also included a section of the western side of Military Road. The order involved every building on the block, including 67 houses, most of which were occupied, in addition to three shops and two public houses. The pubs threatened were 'The Yew Tree' in Military Road, and 'The Union Castle' in Union Street; both Fremlins houses. A third pub, the 'William IV' in Union Street, was not affected and is still there today.

In July 1960 a public enquiry heard objectors to the compulsory purchase and clearance order. Details of this are given on the opposite page. As it happened, all objections were overruled and the buildings were demolished sometime in early 1962.

Redevelopment plans were agreed in November 1962, for what was now being referred to as the Artillery Street – Union Street estate. The council raised no objection to the building of three blocks of flats, 31 garages and a number of old people's flats.

Buffs House on the north side of Artillery Street, as seen in the 'now' picture, is part of the subsequent new development.

(Top photograph courtesy of Canterbury City Council)

ARTILLERY STREET

The four pictures on this page are also part of the same Canterbury City Council commission in June 1960, and show details of further properties along the north side of Artillery Street. The street numbers of each house featured have been written onto the photographs, and both front and rear elevations are shown. The reference numbers probably refer to either the compulsory purchase order or the public enquiry held in June 1960. The enquiry held at the municipal offices heard fourteen objectors to the compulsory purchase and clearance order.

Fremlins Brewery Ltd were represented by Mr J. Girling, who objected to the fact that no alternative sites were to be provided for their two public houses threatened with demolition, namely 'The Union Castle' and 'The Yew Tree'. In response, the council stated that the number of licensed premises remaining in the area would be adequate to meet the local demand.

Most of the other objections heard concerned the terraced houses, including those pictured on this and the opposite page. It was argued that many of the properties could be renovated at a reasonable cost. However, the council called Dr M.S. Harvey, the Medical Officer of Health, who told the enquiry that all of the houses concerned suffered from rising damp, decayed brickwork and pointing and all but one house were without a ventilated food store. Furthermore, the city architect and planner, Mr J.L. Berbiers said that the entire block would need to be demolished, to provide a cleared area of convenient shape and size for redevelopment.

On a more positive note, the council assured objectors that all the residents affected by the order would be given alternative accommodation in the same vicinity. It was also announced that shops would be provided for the traders who would be displaced in the area.

(Courtesy of Canterbury City Council)

LONGMARKET (3)   THE PRE-FABRICATED SHOPS

The third part of the Longmarket feature concentrates on the section of the site towards Butchery Lane. The photograph was taken in early 1959 with The Parade in the foreground, and Butchery Lane visible in the top left part of the picture. By the time this photograph had been taken demolition of the Longmarket site had already begun at the St George's end, but would not reach here until the autumn of 1959.

The pre-fabricated shops appeared in the late 1940s and housed many small businesses displaced in the war. During their ten year existence, the pre-fabs were occupied at various times by the following firms: W.H. Smith & Son, Curtis Quick, E.A. Martyn, H.L. Hambrook, Thanington Court Dairy, Canterbury Galleries, L.W. Bazin, the Sun Café, William Morling Ltd, The National Cash Register Co. Ltd, ADDIS, E.W. Crump, Epworths, National Provincial Bank, Scotch Wool Stores, K.J. Cook, Importers Ltd, C.B. Pettit, A.H. Amey & Son Ltd, and R.E. Cranfield (I apologise for any omissions). Some of these names will be familiar to Canterbury shoppers today.

The pre-fab in the foreground of the picture houses Imports Ltd, tea and coffee specialists. This business found a place in the 'new' Longmarket of the early 1960s, and stayed until 1990 when imminent demolition once again forced them to move. I have always associated the aroma of roasting coffee beans with the Longmarket, and it is something I miss now it is gone.

The fourth version of the Longmarket this century should be finished in the spring of 1992, in time for the fiftieth anniversary of the blitz of Canterbury.

I am grateful to Les Shonk, Manager of Burton, for allowing me access to their balcony, from which the 'now' photograph on this page and on page 16 were taken.

(Fisk-Moore Studio)

The above and below photographs were taken late in 1959, with demolition work in an advanced stage. An almost clear view of the west side of Butchery Lane is now possible. This scene was repeated in the summer of 1990, when the buildings comprising the entire Longmarket early 1960s development were demolished. An extensive archaeological dig uncovered further Roman remains, to add to the mosaic pavement discovered in digs during 1945 and 1946.

The Roman finds will be put on permanent display as part of the new redevelopment of the early 1990s as were the earlier finds, in the 1960s Longmarket scheme.

(Fisk-Moore Studio)

This fascinating photograph of Butchery Lane was taken in 1952. It clearly shows the neat row of pre-fabricated shops along the Long-market side of the lane, with intact pre-war buildings on the other side. Up until 1st June 1942 Butchery Lane was similar to Mercery Lane, in that it was a narrow lane with ancient and interesting buildings on either side. However, the incendiary fires of the blitz of Canterbury were concentrated on the St George's area, and Butchery Lane became a fire break, limiting the spread of destruction westwards. The Longmarket development of the early 1960s produced an imbalanced looking Butchery Lane, with an access yard perimeter wall along much of the Longmarket side. Fortunately, one of the aims of the forthcoming 1991/1992 development will be to recreate the feeling, if not the exact appearance, of the pre-war Butchery Lane.

(Fisk-Moore Studio)

The vast majority of buildings on the Long-market site were demolished during 1959. Many of these were, of course, the pre-fab shops erected at the end of the 1940s. However, despite the fact that the area was devastated in the blitz, there were a few surviving pre-war buildings that were demolished along with the pre-fabs. One such building was the premises of Burton tailors on the corner with Butchery Lane. It can be seen on the left of the picture opposite, as well as in this view dating from September 1959, during the course of demolition. Burtons was once a two-storey building, but the first storey and roof were gutted in the June 1942 bombing. Undaunted, the firm continued to trade from the surviving ground floor portion under a new asbestos roof. This photograph also includes another survivor shortly to be demolished, the old bakehouse, seen just beyond the lorry on the right.

(Fisk-Moore Studio)

THE FIRE OF WESTGATE MILL

In 1930 Canterbury had three large working water mills, all of which have since suffered from serious fires, and from which only one has survived. The first big blaze destroyed Abbotts Mill in February 1933. This stood next to the River Stour on the corner of St Radigund's Street and Mill Lane. Today the site is a popular beer garden, and still contains some mill machinery.

The second fire affected Barton Mill in August 1951. Fortunately, the oldest part of the mill was not involved and survives today as part of a larger industrial complex.

The third big fire destroyed much of Westgate Mill on the night of Tuesday 9th June 1954, and is the subject of the photograph. The mill was made up of three sections: a central timber framed section straddling the water channel, with a brick section on either side. The fire is thought to have broken out in the top floor of the central section at about 10.00 p.m., and quickly spread to the south brick section, seen on the extreme right of the picture.

The blaze was brought under control by 11.25 p.m., although damping down continued into the next day. Firemen managed to save the north brick section, furthest from the camera, which also encompassed an employee's cottage. Unfortunately, the central timber section lost its roof and suffered severe damage to the top floor. Fire damage in the south brick section was worse still. The roof, third and fourth floors were destroyed, and the mill machinery in the entire section was considered a write off.

Although Westgate Mill was subsequently demolished, remains of it could still be found in The Causeway, at the time of writing. The most substantial remnant is a length of wall from the south section, which can clearly be seen in the 'now' photograph. The water channel that formerly ran under the central section is still there, and the large front door step of the north section can still be seen *in situ*, set in the pavement next to a modern street lamp.

(Kentish Gazette)

This view was taken from North Lane and shows the central and southern sections of the mill. The roof of the former section is evidently well alight. Unfortunately, high winds that night had fanned the flames, and the fire spread rapidly. Flames were already bursting through the roofs of the central and southern sections by the time the Canterbury appliances had arrived, despite their prompt turnout.

An urgent message for assistance was quickly sent out, and pumps from Sturry and Bridge were also quickly on the scene. Soon a total of four pumps were in attendance, two in The Causeway and two behind the mill, directing eight jets of water into the inferno. Finally, a turntable ladder was summoned from Dover, and was able to work from above the blazing upper floors and roof of the south section of the mill.

(Kentish Gazette)

The Causeway has always been prone to flooding, especially when the rains of January and February have swollen the River Stour. This photograph was taken in January 1955 from the top end of The Causeway. In the foreground, the water in the Millers Field relief channel can no longer flow under the bridge, and is now coming over the top. This scene was repeated in January 1988, when parts of Canterbury were badly flooded.

The remains of the Westgate Mill can be seen at the far end of The Causeway. The mill owners W. Hooker and Son had, by this time, concentrated all operations on their Chartham Mill. About 50% of the Westgate Mill had been destroyed, and much rebuilding work would need to be done if it was ever to return to business.

(Kentish Gazette)

In the event, Westgate Mill never did operate again. The fire damaged remains lingered on for some months, until the surviving north section was demolished to make way for an improved road junction and pavement between The Causeway and St Stephen's Road.

Apart from the Westgate Mill itself, there were other industrial buildings on the site, including the mill's own detached flour store. All have subsequently been demolished, as has the end wall of the south section of the mill, which clearly still existed in this view dating from around 1960.

A mill is known to have stood here for the best part of a thousand years. Throughout the centuries, the mill has had various names, usually those of its successive owners, including Schepeschotes, Shaffords, Deans and lastly Hookers or Westgate Mill.

(Courtesy of Canterbury City Council)

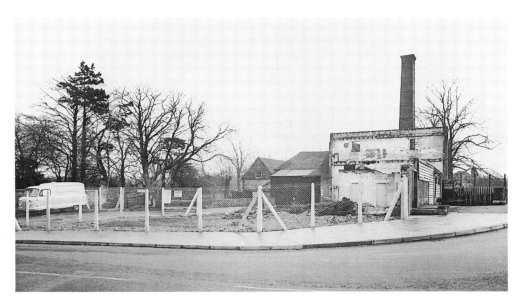

NEW DOVER ROAD
THE DEVELOPMENT OF A CITY BOMB SITE

This fascinating photograph dates from June 1956, and features the crossroads where St George's Place becomes New Dover Road and Chantry Lane crosses from its Upper to Lower sections.

The amazing wide open space, covered in lush summer foliage, was provided courtesy of the Luftwaffe. Prior to this, large elegant buildings occupied the sites on either side of Lower Chantry Lane. On the far corner, and running down almost the entire length of St George's Place, was a superb terrace of three-storey buildings, similar to those surviving on the opposite side. On the corner of Lower Chantry Lane and New Dover Road stood a large red-bricked rectangular four-storey building, that contained, amongst other things, the Citizens Advice Bureau.

In 1956 Lower Chantry Lane was considerably widened, and much later, in 1969, St George's Place became a dual carriageway. Therefore, it could be argued that these buildings would have been demolished anyway had they not perished in the blitz.

In the 1950s the large St George's Place corner site was owned by G.H. Denne & Sons Ltd, and partly by the city council. In March 1961 the council considered selling its part of the site to a private builder for the construction of a block of flats. Nothing came of this plan and in the following year, a temporary car park for fifty vehicles was provided instead. This lasted for twenty years until the Safeway supermarket complex was built.

The New Dover Road site was purchased by Caffyns Ltd in the late 1950s for the construction of a new commercial vehicle showrooms, workshops and stores building. The new complex, opposite their existing main premises, was opened in September 1962. Caffyns have since vacated the building which subsequently changed hands several times. At the time of writing, it was standing empty.

(Fisk-Moore Studio)

Another Fisk-Moore photograph from 1956, this time looking straight down Lower Chantry Lane from the much wider Upper Chantry Lane. In April of that year, the city engineer announced a £13,532 scheme to widen Lower Chantry Lane. This was duly proceeded with and completed in Spring 1957. In June 1957 the East Kent Road Car Co. re-routed their services into and out of the city, along the newly widened road and then into St George's Place. This replaced the previous route of Longport, Church Street, St Paul's and Lower Bridge Street.

(Fisk-Moore Studio)

This picture dates from July 1954, and shows a British Legion parade along New Dover Road. The building behind is, in fact, Legion House. The empty plot of land to the left is the same one featured in the photograph opposite. To the right of Legion House would be the dairy of Abbott Bros (Kent) Ltd at no. 15 New Dover Road, and it is still there today. Legion House was subsequently demolished and the site used, together with the aforementioned empty plot, to build the new showrooms for Caffyns.

(Kentish Gazette)

The main premises of Caffyns Ltd was on the opposite side of New Dover Road on the corner with Upper Chantry Lane, and is pictured here in June 1984, empty and for sale. Up until 1945, these were the premises of Maltby's Ltd, who were the main agents for Morris cars in the area. The building and the business were purchased by Caffyns Ltd in that year. In 1951, Caffyns extended these premises towards the rear.

Today, the building is a furniture superstore for Mammoth, having been extensively altered.

(Kentish Gazette)

ARTILLERY GARDENS
THE DEMISE OF THE OLD ARMY HOUSES

Most of the terraced houses in the Northgate area were built in the early years of the nineteenth century for the families of soldiers stationed in the nearby barracks.

By the 1950s many of these properties had begun to show their age with serious signs of decay. As I have stated elsewhere in the book, it was argued at the time that many of the terraced houses could be renovated at a reasonable cost. However, it must be acknowledged that others were beyond reasonable repair and only fit for the bulldozer. The houses pictured here would appear to come under the latter category. The photograph was taken by the Fisk-Moore Studio in June 1960 and shows nos. 25 to 28 Artillery Gardens, just before demolition. Note that the downstairs windows have been boarded up with internal doors.

Slum clearance in Canterbury was first considered in 1954. By this time the soldiers and their families had long gone and these now decaying properties were mainly occupied by old people. Consequently, when demolition began in earnest in 1959, one of the first priorities was to build old people's bungalows and flats.

Redevelopment of the 'Artillery Gardens Estate' formed part of the 1960 housing programme, which called for the construction of thirty-eight houses and twenty garages in the Northgate area. The 'now' picture shows the block of maisonettes known as Artillery House. It was built in early 1962 with 'special features' provided, according to the housing committee at the time. Consequently, higher-than-average weekly rents were charged. Behind Artillery House is a row of old people's bungalows, built at around the same time. The service road in the foreground was also constructed later in the same year and named Victoria Row, it being an extension of the existing tiny lane of the same name.

(Fisk-Moore Studio)

38

Also taken in June 1960, this picture shows the rear elevation of the same terraced houses in Artillery Gardens. Behind the camera would be Albion Place, featured in the bottom photograph on this page. In August 1960, it was reported that demolition squads, whilst working on the Artillery Gardens properties, had discovered the battered remains of the ancient perimeter wall of St Gregory's Priory. Thirty years later an extensive archaeological dig on the site of the nearby sorting office uncovered much more of the priory itself.

(Fisk-Moore Studio)

This is one of a number of interior photographs taken by Fisk-Moore of no. 27 Artillery Gardens, which is the whitewashed house in the opposite picture. These properties contained none of the facilities we take for granted today, such as internal bathrooms and toilets. Also note that this house had a solid fuel oven. These were amongst things that concerned health officials at the time and helped to hasten the demolition of such properties in the Northgate area.

(Fisk-Moore Studio)

The terraced houses of Albion Place were larger and of more substantial construction than the properties pictured opposite. Albion Place led into Artillery Gardens, and houses from the latter can be seen at the end of the street in this April 1964 view. Artillery Gardens followed an 'L' shape pattern, so that the houses demolished in 1960 would have been behind the left-hand terrace of Albion Place. The Artillery Gardens houses in this view survived until the mid-1960s, whereas the terraced properties on either side of Albion Place survive to this day.

(Kentish Gazette)

LONGMARKET (4)   THE RISE AND FALL OF A SHOEBOX

Until recently, it was unusual to witness both the construction and demolition of a building within a lifetime, let alone thirty years. But now, with plans to redevelop a number of Canterbury's post-war reconstruction sites such as the Longmarket, St George's clock tower and Whitefriars, it is a sight that will become increasingly more familiar.

The photograph dates from 1960 and shows the framework for the Longmarket's infamous 'shoebox' tower block being erected. Plans for this and the other proposed Longmarket buildings were approved by the city council in February 1958. However, the plans met with strong disapproval from other quarters. In early 1959 a petition, organised by the English-speaking Union, called for the scrapping of the plan to build the four-storey 'Longmarket monstrosity'. Signatories, and other objectors including the Dean and Chapter, disliked the 'matchbox' because it prevented a clear view of the cathedral. Unfortunately some less well informed signatories stated that they wanted to see the area as it was before the blitz, when 'there had been a wonderful view of the cathedral!'

In defence of the plans, the mayor Alderman W.S. Bean who was also on the planning committee stated that, contrary to what some of the signatories thought, the old pre-war Longmarket roof had been higher than the proposed four-storey block. Moreover, the so-called 'matchbox' would be no taller than the two banks beside it. With regards to the Dean and Chapter's involvement, Mr Bean remarked that if they were so concerned about unobstructed views of the cathedral, why did they rebuild Burgate?

Construction went ahead and progressed well throughout 1960, with the objective of having most of the shops trading by that Christmas.

Thirty years later, official opinions have changed, and the much criticised buildings are coming down. The hoardings are back up as they were in 1960, and a different generation of Canterbury people take a passing interest in what is going on.

(Messenger Group Newspapers)

The final development plans for the Long-market area were drawn up by the city architect's department in January 1958, and approved by the Canterbury City Council the following month. Details of the new development sounded very exciting with mention of such features as a continental style roof terrace and two covered arcades linking Butchery Lane with the new square. Most of the announced details actually made it into the finished product, and the new Longmarket development that emerged in the early 1960s was remarkably similar in appearance to the city architect's artwork, reproduced here. However, I wonder what happened to the pond and ornamental fountain in the middle of the square?

(Kentish Gazette from a city architect's dept. drawing)

The new buildings on the right of this picture were constructed between 1955 and 1958. They stretch from the National Provincial Bank building in the foreground, down to Burgate at the far end. Although facing into the Long-market, they were not part of the actual Longmarket plan as detailed above and on the opposite page. In June 1958, the city council wanted the building work in the Longmarket redevelopment area to begin by January 1959. They hoped that the area would be cleared of most of the old buildings by that date. In the event, this forecast proved to be too optimistic. Demolition of the prefabricated shops and the few pre-war buildings on the Longmarket site did not actually begin until January 1959. By the time this photograph was taken in February a number of pre-fabs from the plot in the centre of the picture had already gone. Other buildings and pre-fabs on the left await a similar fate.

(Kentish Gazette)

However the new Longmarket four-storey block was described, be it a matchbox, shoebox or monstrosity, it was never very complimentary! This south-looking view of the new development was taken in October 1961. In the same month, the new Longmarket was officially opened, although many of the shops had already been open for business for some months. The more usual north-looking view of the new Longmarket can be found on the back cover, and makes an interesting comparison to the planned drawing at the top of this page.

As can be seen from this photograph, seats and benches were installed right from the start. The flowering cherry trees were added during the following year.

(Kentish Gazette)

LONGPORT   THE OLD HOSPITAL THAT BECAME A SCHOOL

This picture from May 1952 features Longport and a large building which, under various guises, served the people of Canterbury for the best part of 200 years.

The large central section of the building started life in 1793 as the Kent and Canterbury Hospital. It was built on three acres of land within the grounds of St Augustine's Monastery, on what was once a lay cemetery. Extension wings on either side of the original structure were added in 1828 and 1838. Further extensions and improvements came over the next 100 years, the last being the opening of children's wards in a series of outbuildings in 1933.

A new hospital along Ethelbert Road was opened in June 1937, and the old buildings sold. A new use was subsequently found in 1941, when the Technical Institute was established. However, the needs of wartime Canterbury saw yet another use for the building as an emergency rest centre, capable of accommodating 200 people. Many people who became homeless as a result of the raids in June and October 1942 were glad of the temporary shelter it provided. In peacetime, the building reverted to entirely educational purposes encompassing the Technical College and Technical School for Boys. The school was for boys from the age of thirteen to sixteen, with pupils divided into four educational courses, namely building, agricultural, engineering and general.

A new Technical High School for Boys was opened in the autumn of 1967, later to be known as the 'Geoffrey Chaucer'. The Technical College hung on in the old buildings, until its activities were transferred to the present complex just off New Dover Road. The old buildings were finally demolished in 1972. The only consolation for the loss is the establishment of a pleasing garden on the site, from which wonderful views of the adjacent abbey ruins may be enjoyed.

(Fisk-Moore Studio)

This was the scene at the Longport coach park one Sunday in April 1955, when Mr F.C. Braby, the County Commissioner, inspected Canterbury and District Scouts and Guides taking part in the St George's Day parade. Much of the Technical Institute complex can be seen along Longport in the background.

The coach park was once a densely developed area containing two further schools. Unfortunately, bombing in the June 1942 blitz levelled the entire background.

(Kentish Gazette)

This is a much later view of the Boys' Tech, dating from October 1965. The trees have grown considerably since the photograph opposite was taken, and many of them are still there today, although the building is gone.

Contrary to popular belief, the old Tech building was not the exclusive domain of the male sex. Girls from the Technical High School opposite regularly used the facilities here, particularly when examinations were held. The Girls' Tech is now known as the Barton Court School.

(Kentish Gazette)

The old Kent and Canterbury Hospital buildings were purchased in 1939, with the expressed intention of eventually pulling them down to 're-unite once again the old graveyard with the abbey precinct'. In the meantime, they were leased to the city council for use as a Technical Institute. Demolition finally came in 1972, and was completed by June of that year when this photograph was taken. A subsequent archaeological dig of the site uncovered many ancient burials and two silver pennies of pre-conquest date.

(Kentish Gazette)

LOWER BRIDGE STREET (2)
THE OLD AND NEW INVICTA PREMISES

The Invicta Motor Engineering Works Ltd was founded in 1922 and operated out of premises in Lower Bridge Street. Adjacent properties were subsequently purchased to extend the complex, as the company expanded to meet the increasing demand for motor vehicles. This photograph, from Invicta's own collection, shows how the premises appeared in the 1950s, as a variety of buildings of different ages, shapes and sizes. By 1957 the piecemeal nature of Invicta's premises were no longer suitable for the efficient running of a modern motor company. In that same year, the Ford Motor Company forecast a significant growth of the car population. Taking these two facts into account, Invicta decided to modernise the entire complex. This involved the progressive demolition of the existing collection of buildings sandwiched between St George's Post Office and Brickies of Kent, butchers.

The new premises were designed by a Canterbury architect, Mr John Clague. They were to be built in three distinct and separate phases to minimise disruption of business on the site. Work started towards the end of 1961, and the new premises were officially opened in September 1963.

In 1974 Invicta bought the aforementioned premises of Brickies, next to its new complex, for use as office accommodation. Later on, this former butcher's shop was demolished and replaced by a purpose built office suite. However, it continued to be referred to as 'Brickie's' by Invicta staff for many years afterwards. Recently, Invicta sold the entire Lower Bridge Street site, to join with the commercial vehicle sector in a vast new complex along Sturry Road.

The former premises have now been refurbished and divided into individual shop units.

(Top photograph reproduced by kind permission of Invicta Motor Co.)

This view from November 1954 clearly shows just how much the A28 narrowed as it changed from Broad Street in the foreground to Lower Bridge Street. The 'Saracen's Head' on the right (see also pages 28 and 29) became an inevitable casualty of road improvements in 1969.

The premises of Invicta Motors can be seen along the left side of Lower Bridge Street. They had survived the blitz of Canterbury intact, but were nearly razed to the ground in 1949, when the driver of a visiting petrol tanker lit a cigarette while unloading. The unfortunate fellow did not survive, but local firemen managed to contain the resultant blaze.

(Kentish Gazette)

This picture dates from around November 1962, by which time stage one of the redevelopment had been completed. It can just be seen furthest away from the camera. Stage one provided half the total administrative office space, a ground floor second-hand car showroom, and workshops on the first floor. Stages two and three were constructed simultaneously. The steel frames for this phase had already been erected, and can be seen sandwiched between the finished stage one and the premises of Brickies of Kent. The used car lot between Brickies and Ivy Lane would subsequently be given up, and provide a site for the new Royal Insurance building.

(Photograph reproduced by kind permission of Invicta Motor Co.)

The finished product as seen in October 1964, just over a year after stages two and three had been completed, and the whole new complex officially opened. Stage two fronted onto Lower Bridge Street and comprised further workshop and administrative areas as well as the main showrooms, petrol service station, stores and reception. Stage three was positioned behind stage two and linked it to the one remaining building from the old complex. This last stage provided further workshop areas on both floors.

This photograph also gives us a good view of Brickies butcher's shop, which would later be purchased by Invicta.

(Kentish Gazette)

CANTERBURY LANE   THE BATTLE OF THE BAKERY

The post-war development plan for Canterbury required that certain areas of the blitzed city be redeveloped as whole blocks. This was considered preferable to allowing the pre-war freehold or leasehold owners to rebuild on a piecemeal basis. Compulsory purchase was therefore a necessary part of this process. Thus, street straightening and widening could more easily be planned and architects allowed to work on larger more uniform designs. Consequently, there was little allowance made for the few buildings that had survived the blitz and those in the St George's area were amongst the first buildings to be demolished since the war. Loyn's Bakery in Canterbury Lane was an early victim. Designed by architect Harold Anderson, this 'modern' machine bakery was built in 1928 at a cost of £3,680.

Amazingly, it survived the intense blitz of June 1942, largely due to its solid modern construction and flat roof. In 1951 Arthur Loyn sold the business to Nicholas Kingsman Ltd, but only three years later, a bitter wrangle developed over the bakery's impending compulsory purchase.

The proprietor, E.E. Kingsman, who was also a councillor at the time, quite rightly withdrew from any negotiations on the side of the city council. However, as a business man he fought to be allowed to either keep Loyn's Bakery, or be offered suitable premises elsewhere. In January 1954 a site in St George's Place, next to the new Kentish Gazette buildings, was offered for the erection of a new bakery. But time was running out. The compulsory purchase order was pushed through in June 1954 and Loyn's Bakery demolished in the following month.

The area around St George's clock tower, including the former site of Loyn's Bakery, was subsequently developed by Ravenseft. (They had previously been responsible for the south side of St George's Street.) These shops, which date from 1955, were themselves demolished late in 1990, to allow a denser redevelopment that will come much closer to the old clock tower.

(Kentish Gazette)

The photograph opposite was a selective enlargement of Loyn's Bakery, taken from a more general view of the area. I thought it worth reproducing the original picture as well, as it nicely illustrates how the old bakery was gradually being surrounded by the new post-war buildings of Canterbury as they spread along St George's Street. In the foreground, workmen are laying the foundations for the Canterbury Lane parking area, on the site of St George's churchyard. To the left, scaffolding surrounds the old clock tower of St George's Church, then undergoing restoration.

(Kentish Gazette)

Close-up pictures of Loyn's Bakery are few and far between, although it quite often appears in the background on other photographs of post-war Canterbury. This view of the front of the 'machine bakery' in Canterbury Lane appeared in the Kentish Gazette around the time the compulsory purchase dispute first flared up. Unfortunately the original negative has been lost and this is a copy from the paper itself, hence the poorer quality. New buildings from the Ravenseft no. 1 development can be seen along the south side of St George's Street.

(Kentish Gazette via Mr E.E. Kingsman)

This view was taken from the newly formed junction into St George's Lane and looking across St George's Street. It dates from July 1954, by which time restoration of St George's clock tower was almost complete, with only the clock itself awaiting reinstatement. The brand new award winning David Greig building can be seen on the west side of Canterbury Lane. On the lane's eastern side and visible to the right of the clock tower is the sad sight of Loyn's Bakery being demolished. Compensation paid for the leasehold interest of the bakery was £6,000. The cost of building a similar bakery elsewhere would have been £10,500.

(Kentish Gazette)

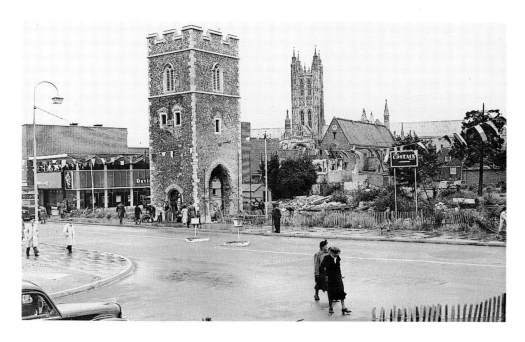

CASTLE STREET (2)
THE MOVEMENT OF A FIRM OUT OF CANTERBURY

Forty years ago there were quite a number of building and manufacturing firms based in the centre of Canterbury. Over the years, most have either ceased to trade or have relocated to purpose-built industrial estates on the outskirts of the city. Cakebread, Robey and Co. Ltd come under the latter category, and this photograph shows part of their old business premises in Castle Street. The picture was taken in June 1949 and shows a single-storey display building containing bottled gas appliances. To the left of this were some gates, a three-storey showroom and office building also fronting Castle Street. The yard extended round into Adelaide Place and gave access to other buildings, including an old corrugated iron store for builders' materials.

In the late 1960s and early 1970s many firms were encouraged to move out of the city. This was for a variety of reasons, amongst them the inability of Canterbury's narrow streets to cope with the new generation of larger lorries being used. In early 1973, Cakebread, Robey and Co. Ltd moved to Wincheap industrial estate, and the vast majority of their old premises were demolished. The narrow two-storey building seen to the right of the 1949 photograph was also demolished. The site remained vacant behind hoardings for a period, until redeveloped in the late 1970s.

Two new buildings emerged, and can be seen in the 'now' picture. The kitchen showrooms is a pleasing modern building, whilst the estate agent to its left is a clever reconstruction of the aforementioned three-storey showroom building once belonging to Cakebread Robey.

I am grateful to Bob Lumley and Geoff Shaxted of Cakebread Robey for their help in compiling this feature.

(Fisk-Moore Studio)